GREG MADDUX

MASTER ON THE MOUND

BY BILL GUTMAN

Millbrook Sports World
The Millbrook Press
Brookfield, Connecticut

Cover photographs courtesy of © Allsport USA (Otto Greule; inset Jed Jacobsohn)

Photographs courtesy of © Allsport USA: pp. 3 (Jonathan Daniel), 4 (Otto Greule), 33 (Matthew Stockman), 35 (Doug Pensinger), 40 (Jonathan Daniel); Seth Poppel Yearbook Archives: pp. 10, 11; Peoria Journal Star: p. 14; Corbis/Bettmann-UPI: p. 18; AP/Wide World Photos: pp. 21, 25, 27, 37; SportsChrome-USA: p. 44 (© 1997 Jeff Carlick); Reuters/Corbis-Bettmann: p. 46

Library of Congress Cataloging-in-Publication Data
Gutman, Bill.
Greg Maddux : master on the mound / Bill Gutman.
p. cm. — (Millbrook sports world)
Includes bibliographical references and index.
Summary: Follows the life of baseball pitcher Greg Maddux, from his childhood in an Air Force family to his career with the Chicago Cubs and Atlanta Braves.
ISBN 0-7613-1454-7 (lib. bdg.)
1. Maddux, Greg (1966–   )—Juvenile literature. 2. Baseball players—United States—Biography—Juvenile literature. 3. Pitchers (Baseball)—United States—Biography—Juvenile literature. [1. Maddux, Greg (1966–   ) . 2. Baseball players.] I. Title. II. Series.
GV865.M233G88   1999
796.357'092—dc21
[B]   99-12812   CIP

Published by The Millbrook Press, Inc.
2 Old New Milford Road
Brookfield, Connecticut 06804
www.millbrookpress.com

GREG
MADDUX

Greg Maddux's Atlanta Braves teammates congratulate him after his spectacular pitching performance in the first game of the 1995 World Series. With Greg's help, Atlanta would go on to beat the Cleveland Indians in the Series.

The first game of the World Series is very important. To each team, it is crucial to win the opener. If possible, each team wants its best pitcher ready to go. From that standpoint, the opening game of the 1995 World Series looked to be a classic. The American League Cleveland Indians were starting veteran pitcher Orel Hershiser. He had a 16–6 record during the regular season, and a 7–0 career record in postseason play.

Opposing the Indians were the National League Atlanta Braves. Despite Hershiser's presence, the Braves were favored, largely because of their starting pitcher. Right-hander Greg Maddux had just completed an incredible season in which he had achieved an amazing 19–2 record and 1.63 earned run average. But 1995 wasn't Greg's first outstanding year. He had won the Cy Young Award, given to the league's best pitcher, the past three years and was the overwhelming favorite to win it an unprecedented fourth straight time. In the eyes of many, he had become the best pitcher in baseball.

As expected, the game was a pitcher's duel. Cleveland scored an unearned run in the first inning on an error, followed by two stolen bases and a groundout. Atlanta tied it in the second on a long home run by Fred McGriff. Then the pitchers took over. Hershiser kept the Braves at bay for the next four innings, but Maddux was even better. After the unearned run in the first, the Indians looked more like Little Leaguers than the American League's best.

Standing an even 6 feet (183 centimeters) tall and weighing a modest 175 pounds (79 kilograms), Greg Maddux doesn't look like a typical intimidating pitcher of the 1990s. He doesn't overpower opposing hitters. Rather, he out-thinks them. Using his great control and a variety of speeds and movements, he concentrates on making good pitches. More often than not, the pitches he throws are not the ones the hitter expects. That's what the Cleveland batters learned the hard way during the first game of the 1995 World Series.

The game was still tied at 1–1 in the bottom of the seventh inning. When Hershiser walked the first two batters, he was removed from the game. Atlanta went on to score two runs against the relief pitchers to take a 3–1 lead.

It was still 3-1 going into the ninth. Greg had given up just one hit. Then with one out, Cleveland's Kenny Lofton singled. He raced around to third and came in to score on a wild throw by first baseman Fred McGriff. Again, the run was unearned. Then Greg closed it out by getting Carlos Baerga to pop out to third. The Braves had won it 3–2 with Maddux throwing a masterpiece.

Pitching in all nine innings, Greg had given up just two hits. He didn't walk a single batter and he struck out four. Had it not been for the errors his team committed, he would have pitched a shutout. His teammates, of course, were used to this kind of game from him. Cleveland Manager Mike Hargrove quickly came to realize what players in Maddux's own league had known for years. "I've been around this game a long time," Hargrove said. "That was as well a pitched game as I think I've ever seen. [Greg] is everything you'd want a pitcher to be. He totally dominated this game."

A TRAVELING AIR-FORCE KID

Children who have parents in the military often move around while they are growing up. They may travel from military base to military base within the United States and even live overseas for a time. Since his father was in the United States Air Force, that is the way Greg Maddux grew up.

He was born in San Angelo, Texas, on April 14, 1966, the third child of Dave and Linda Maddux. Greg's sister, Terri, was seven years older and his brother, Mike, was four years older.

Greg's father loved to play fast-pitch softball. Wherever he was transferred, he immediately joined the air-force base team. He also began teaching his children how to play baseball as soon as they were old enough to walk. He taught them all the phases of the game—throwing, batting, fielding, and pitching. If they were going to play the game, he wanted them to know how to play it right.

Greg worked hard to keep up with his older brother. Sometimes Mike and his friends didn't want young Greg playing with them. But as Greg got older, he soon showed the bigger kids that he knew how to play and could keep up with them. Meanwhile, the family continued to move around. They lived in Texas, Indiana, North Dakota, California, and then went to Europe to live in Spain.

It wasn't always easy to make friends in a new place, but there was always baseball. There were more than enough kids on all the air-force bases to get up a game. Baseball became the easiest way for the Maddux kids to make new friends. The family stayed in Spain longer than the other places they had lived. That's where both Maddux boys played Little League.

By the time Greg was old enough to join a Little League team, he was also good enough to start. He was in the lineup against boys two and three years older. All the work he had done to keep up with his brother, Mike, and the older kids had paid off for Greg. Both Greg and Mike excelled on their Little League teams.

When Greg was ten years old, his father was transferred again. He was assigned to a base in Las Vegas, Nevada. This time the family would stay. Las Vegas may be considered the gambling capital of the world, but it also has a warm climate where baseball can be played all year round.

In Las Vegas, Mike and Greg Maddux received the final touches on their baseball education.

The man who helped with this was Rusty Medar. He was a former big-league scout who loved to teach baseball and help young players develop. He invited promising youngsters to attend his informal practice sessions on Sundays. Medar enjoyed giving youngsters the benefits of his many years in the game, but he wanted only players who were serious and showed real promise. Mike Maddux was one of these players.

Soon after the family moved to Las Vegas, Rusty Medar asked the four-teen-year-old Mike to begin coming to his practices. Mike, of course, was ex-cited. He couldn't wait to play. His father, Dave, and younger brother, Greg, tagged along to watch. Mike became a regular at Medar's Sunday sessions, and Greg was always there as well, playing catch on the sidelines or throwing with the older boys before the sessions began. It wasn't long before the retired scout asked Greg to join in.

Even at eleven years of age, Greg had a smooth pitching motion. More than that, however, Medar couldn't help noticing how consistent Greg's pitches were—he released the ball from exactly the same spot every time. The coach couldn't believe a young boy could be so consistent. "Your son has great mechanics," Medar told Greg's father. "Don't let anyone change him."

Greg continued to join in the Sunday sessions. Even though college players and local pros showed up in the winter, Greg hung in there. He was always the youngest player in the group, but he was used to playing with older people and it didn't bother him. Whenever Greg pitched, Medar stood alongside him, giving him advice.

He told Greg that pitching was more than just throwing the ball hard. He emphasized that pinpoint control could be a pitcher's best weapon. Throwing strikes wasn't always the most important thing, but throwing the ball where you wanted to throw it was. In addition, he advised Greg not to try throwing curveballs too soon—many youngsters hurt their arms that way. Instead, he taught Greg how to throw the change-up, a slower pitch that is released with the same motion as a fastball. That pitch would become one of Greg's major assets years later.

HEADING FOR THE MINOR LEAGUES

Mike was the first of the Maddux brothers to show flashes of future baseball stardom. It began at Valley High School in Las Vegas. Mike was a lanky 6-foot-2-inch (188-centimeter) right-handed pitcher, and by the time he was a senior he was one of the stars of the team. He was so good, in fact, that he was drafted by the boys' favorite team, the Cincinnati Reds. But Mike listened to the advice of his father and Rusty Medar and accepted a scholarship to the University of Texas at El Paso instead.

Greg, in the meantime, continued to improve. In addition to baseball, he excelled at basketball. In the summers he worked at a local fast-food restaurant making hamburgers. In 1980 he followed his brother Mike to Valley High.

Valley High's baseball coach, Roger Fairless, was an outstanding mentor who had sent a number of his players on to professional careers. But for two years Greg didn't play much, and had not cracked the starting lineup. It was during that time that he received some advice from old friend Rusty Medar that

By the time he entered high school in the early 1980s, Greg was developing as a great pitcher. By the time he was a senior (facing page), Greg had good reason to smile; major-league scouts were already taking notice. In the team photo below, Greg is at the far right in the back row.

may have changed his baseball future.

Greg knew he couldn't throw as hard as some of the bigger, stronger boys. But Medar told him to stop worrying about that. "You're probably never going to throw hard enough to overpower people," Medar said. He then suggested that Greg change the point at which he released his pitches. The change worked. A slightly lower arm angle and a different grip before releasing a fastball immediately made Greg's pitches trickier for hitters. Instead of moving straight, the fastball now danced down and away from left-handed hitters.

Greg Maddux

Though back problems prevented Greg from pitching a lot as a junior, he nevertheless became an important part of the team, playing center field. He hit a grand-slam home run in the league championship game and was named to the All-State team.

Brother Mike had been drafted by the Philadelphia Phillies out of college and was in the minor leagues as Greg began his senior year at Valley High in the fall of 1983. Though Greg didn't know it at the time, Chicago Cubs scout Ray Handley had made a mental note of Greg's work and asked a local scout to keep an eye on him.

In his senior season Greg's fastball measured more than 80 miles (129 kilometers) per hour. While that was not superfast, it was more than enough to handle many high-school hitters, especially when the pitches moved as well as Greg's. As Coach Fairless would say later: "The thing that always made Greg different was his control and poise on the mound. He just never got behind or in trouble."

Throughout Greg's senior year the scouts came and watched. Their only concern was his size. Had he weighed a solid 200 pounds (91 kilograms), he might have been a first-round draft choice. But at a slight 145 pounds (66 kilograms), he would probably go much lower. Soon it was apparent that Greg would have to make the same decision as his brother: sign with a professional team or go to college. He already had a scholarship offer from the University of Arizona, which had one of the best collegiate baseball programs in the country.

The 1984 major-league draft was held on June 4. At the time, Greg was in Hawaii with his Valley High classmates for their senior trip. It wasn't until he returned home that he learned the Chicago Cubs had made him the third pick of the second round of the draft. He was the thirty-first player taken in the entire country. Now the question was what to do.

Greg thought about it. He had done well in high school and had always planned to go to college. But by this time he loved baseball and pitching enough to know that he wanted a shot at the major leagues. He knew there were already several fine pitchers ahead of him at Arizona. If he went there, it might take two years before he could become a starter. In the minors, he'd be pitching immediately.

What if he hurt his arm at college? Then his major-league dream would be gone forever. The clincher, however, was the Cubs offer of an $85,000 bonus. To eighteen-year-old Greg, that seemed like a fortune. Finally, he struck a bargain with his parents. He promised not to touch the bonus money until he reached the major leagues. If he didn't make it, he would have the money to put himself through college and get started in another profession.

His parents agreed and Greg signed with the Cubs. He was immediately assigned to the Cubs's single-A minor-league team at Pikeville, North Carolina, of the Appalachian League. He was now a professional baseball player.

A FAST ROAD TO THE MAJORS

Greg left Las Vegas to join his new teammates in June 1984. Like other young players just out of high school, he suddenly found himself alone, thousands of miles from home. He had to make new friends, listen to a manager and coaches, and face tougher competition. But Greg Maddux had advantages over the others.

Being an air-force kid had made Greg used to moving around and adjusting to new places. Furthermore, he had an older brother already in the minors who had been telling him all along what to expect and how to handle it. He and Mike talked often and soon were helping and encouraging each other.

Another of Greg's advantages was his pitching. Many young pitchers are hard throwers who have great difficulty getting their pitches under control. But Greg came to the minors with the fine control he had developed in high school— and it was only getting better.

Not surprisingly, he was outstanding in the short Pikeville season. He made 14 appearances, starting 12 times, and wound up with a record of 6–2.

He threw a pair of shutouts and had a fine earned run average of 2.63. The Cubs were more than pleased with their second-round acquisition. They wanted to see more of Greg and in the off-season sent him to pitch in the Arizona Instructional League.

Facing even better hitters in Arizona than he had seen in the Appalachian League, Greg's earned run average was a skimpy 1.88 in 29 innings. In the spring of 1985 the Cubs sent him to their Peoria, Illinois, team in the Midwest League. It was still single-A baseball, but at a higher level than Pikeville. At the beginning of the 1986 season, they sent him to Pittsfield, Massachusetts, to pitch in the double-A Eastern League.

Greg made 8 starts at Pittsfield. His record was just 4–3, but he had thrown a pair of shutouts and had a low 2.69 earned run average. The Cubs then promoted him to their Iowa team in the American Association. He had reached the triple-A level, the highest in the minor leagues. His next stop would be the majors.

In triple A, he was outstanding again. In 18 starts, he compiled a 10–1 record and a 3.02 ERA. In his August starts from that season, his earned run average was an anemic 1.60.

On September 1 of each baseball season, big-league teams can expand their rosters and bring up the minor leaguers they want to have a taste of the majors.

During Greg's stint with the Peoria, Illinois, Chiefs in 1985 he racked up a 13–9 record and a 3.19 earned run average over 186 innings, and struck out 125 batters while walking only 52. More and more he was beginning to look like big-league material at just 20 years of age.

When the call was made to Iowa, Greg Maddux was one of the players called up. At the age of twenty, Greg was in the major leagues.

BATTLING SOME EARLY DEMONS

The Chicago Cubs were one of baseball's classic franchises, having represented the same city in the major leagues longer than any other club besides the Cincinnati Reds. But the Cubs hadn't won a World Series since 1908. So when Greg joined the team at the end of the 1986 season, long suffering, loyal Cubs fans were still hoping for a championship.

The team played at Wrigley Field, one of the oldest and smallest ballparks in the majors. It was known as a hitter's park, with relatively short outfield walls. But that didn't bother Greg. He was in the big leagues. That's what meant the most to him.

The Cubs had won the National League East title in 1984, but had since fallen back. When Greg came up, Chicago was in fifth place, some thirty games behind the division-leading New York Mets. Greg played in six games in September. He started five times but had a 2–4 record and an unimpressive 5.52 earned run average.

The high point of his introduction to the majors was his first start against Cincinnati. Greg pitched the whole game for an 11–3 victory, his first big-league win. In Greg's other victory, he beat the Philadelphia Phillies 8–3, pitching 7.2 innings. The losing pitcher for Philly was his brother, Mike. "I would have liked to [see] Mike do better," Greg said, "but I'm just glad we won. I look forward to any game, but this one [against Mike] was a little more fun."

In 1987, Greg began the season as the Cubs' fifth starter. Now he would have to sink or swim against the best players in the world. One of his minor-league coaches saw him as a good big-league pitcher, but not a superstar. "Greg is not a strikeout pitcher and probably won't ever win twenty-five or thirty games," the coach said. "But he should have a good big-league career."

That career didn't get off to a flying start in 1987. In fact, Greg almost became his own worst enemy that year. He began getting angry at the smallest thing. Maybe it was a pitch that didn't go where he wanted. Maybe it was a close call by an umpire that didn't go his way. When those things happened, he yelled at himself, the umpires, and the other hitters. His teammates gave him the most unlikely of nicknames—Mad Dog.

At twenty years of age, Greg was the youngest player in the majors that year and he still needed to grow up in many ways. For one thing, Greg's fastball wasn't improving. Sometimes he could get it up to 90 miles (145 kilometers) per hour. But when he threw the ball as hard as he could, it flew to the plate straight as an arrow, making it very easy to hit. Yet he continued throwing these fastballs, and the hitters began having a field day. Not surprisingly, Greg began to lose.

When his record fell to 6–10 and his earned run average climbed to almost 5.00, the Cubs knew they had to do something. The team felt the solution was to return Greg to the minor leagues.

Back in Iowa, he regained his dominance, winning three of the four games he started, throwing a pair of shutouts, and compiling an 0.98 earned run average. Two weeks later he was back with the Cubs.

Once again, however, he couldn't win. It was as if he were two different pitchers. In the minors he was unbeatable. At the big-league level he couldn't win. Even Greg admitted later that in 1987 he had no idea what was going on. "I didn't really understand anything about pitching then," he said, "and I didn't un-derstanding anything about acting like a pitcher."

Greg lost four more games before the season ended and finished the year with a dismal 6–14 mark. He had just a single complete game in 27 starts and an earned run average of 5.61. He gave up 181 hits in just 155.2 innings of work and even walked 74 hitters. It was questionable whether he would even make the team in 1988.

That winter, Greg followed the suggestion of the Cubs that he play winter ball in the South American country of Venezuela. Accompanying him was Dick Pole, his minor-league pitching coach at Iowa. Pole knew there had to be some major changes in order to harness Greg's natural talent and intelligence. The two began working together every day.

The only interruption in the schedule came when Greg returned to Las Vegas between games to get married. His wife, Kathy, had been his high-school sweetheart. Now they faced the future together and hoped it would be in baseball.

FINDING STARDOM

Back in Venezuela, Greg continued to work with Dick Pole. They spent hours just talking about pitching; how to formulate a game plan and how to think about each individual hitter and come up with the best way to get him out. Also, Greg knew that he had to lose his "Mad Dog" image.

Greg's first season in the major leagues was a disappointment. But by the time this picture was taken during the 1989 season, he had improved drastically and even finished third in the voting for the Cy Young Award.

When he returned to Chicago for the 1988 season Greg showed immediately that he was a changed person, and a different kind of pitcher. His first start of the season came on April 6 against the Atlanta Braves. His fastball was a success, and his change-up kept the Braves' hitters off balance all game. When it ended, Greg had a three-hit shutout and the Cubs won 3–0. "The credit for this belongs to Dick Pole," Greg said afterward. "Last year it was one fastball after another. Not any more. Dick Pole can teach you a lot of different things."

Greg soon showed that his opener hadn't been a fluke. He continued winning and pitching as well as anyone in baseball. By the end of May, the twenty-two-year-old right-hander had an 8–3 record and what suddenly seemed like an unlimited future ahead of him.

By the time the All-Star Game rolled around in early July, Greg had an amazing 15–3 record and, not surprisingly, was picked as one of the National League pitchers. "I can't tell you how happy I am to be selected," he said. "This was something I never thought about before. You don't think about the All-Star team when you were 6–14 the year before." Greg didn't get to pitch in the All-Star Game, which the American League won 2–1. But he was happy to be there among the greatest players in the game.

Having just achieved the fiftieth win of his career the week before, Greg throws a pitch in a July 1990 game against the St. Louis Cardinals. The fiftieth win seemed to turn that season around for Greg, who had a poor 4–9 record until then.

If the first half of the season was a revelation, the second half was a disappointment. From his 15–3 record at the All-Star break, he could only muster a 3–5 mark for the rest of the season to finish at 18–8.

It was still a huge improvement from the year before. Greg had completed 9 of his 34 starts, struck out 140 batters in 249 innings, walked just 81, and had a fine earned run average of 3.18. At last, it seemed he was a pitcher with a bright future. Now he hoped to find consistency over a full season.

For the next three seasons, Greg Maddux looked like a pitcher on the brink of stardom. In 1989 he had a 19–12 record as the Cubs surprised everyone by winning the National League's Eastern Division.

Although the Cubs were beaten in the play-offs by the San Francisco Giants, it had been a good year for Greg. His earned run average was under 3.00 (at 2.95) for the first time in the majors, and he threw 7 complete games in 35 starts. He finished third in the voting for the Cy Young Award, given to the league's best pitcher. His reward was a new contract that would pay him $2.4 million in 1990.

The 1990 season was almost the reverse of 1988. This time, he got off to a horrendous start. Greg made 13 straight starts without a victory, going 0–8 during that period. He was 4–9 on July 18, when he beat the San Diego Padres, 4–2, for the 50th win of his young career. That game seemed to turn things around. He won five straight games and again looked like one of the best.

Greg also achieved something new that year—he won the Gold Glove Award as the best fielding pitcher in the league. It was an award he would continue to win throughout the 1990s.

In 1991, Greg put together a 15–11 record in 37 starts. He worked a career-high 263 innings and had a career-best 198 strikeouts. His earned run average was still a mediocre 3.35, but he won another Gold Glove. The Cubs, however, were in fourth place and out of the race for the championship.

Greg's contract was up at the end of 1991, and it was time to make some decisions about the future. He still wanted to improve as a pitcher, but he had yet another goal, one for his entire team. "I want to pitch in the World Series," he said. "I dream about it."

THE CY YOUNG AWARD AND A NEW TEAM

Greg was just twenty-five years old at the end of the 1991 season. He had won 67 games over four years. With his contract up, he felt he now wanted a long-term deal. But the Cubs didn't agree. They said Greg simply had not been consistent enough for a multiyear contract. Still, Greg signed a very big one-year pact. He would be paid $4.2 million to pitch in 1992. If he had another good year, he would have a choice: re-sign with the Cubs or test the open market as a free agent.

The Cubs didn't have a good team in 1992. It was apparent after just a few months that they wouldn't be contending for the division title. Greg, however, was pitching very well without getting a lot of run support. At the All-Star break he had a 10–8 record, and his earned run average was just over 2.00. This time, he not only made the All-Star team, but pitched in the game for the first time.

He also made a decision before the second half of the season began. Feeling that the Cubs simply weren't in a position to contend for a title, he made an announcement that some found surprising. "I've decided to become a free agent at the end of the year," he said. "Let's just say I'm a bit disappointed at the way things have gone here."

It's unusual for a ballplayer to announce his intentions at midyear. Of course, the Cubs could bid for Greg's services along with everyone else. But it was felt by most that Greg's days in Chicago would soon be over.

During the second half of the 1992 season, he went out to the mound every five days and pitched the best baseball of his life. In his final start of the year, Greg shut out the Pittsburgh Pirates for his 20th victory, a milestone that all pitchers look forward to achieving. His final mark was 20–11, with a 2.18 earned run average, 199 strikeouts, 268 innings pitched, 4 shutouts, and 9 complete games. All these marks tied or established Greg's career bests. His 35 starts and 268 innings pitched led the National League.

Shortly after the season ended, Greg Maddux was named the winner of the Cy Young Award. Despite pitching for a team that finished fourth, his peers considered him the best in the league. He had truly come a long way. "Winning this [award] means a lot to me personally," Greg said. "It means that all the hard work over the years has finally paid off. The only thing left is for me to pitch in the World Series."

Now the question was: Where would Greg be pitching in 1993? This time the Cubs made a five-year offer worth $27.5 million with an incentive package worth another million. But Greg said he was thinking more about winning and turned the Cubs down. He would look for a stronger team.

He was then courted by the New York Yankees. They offered him an amazing six-year deal worth $37.5 million. It was the largest contract ever offered any player at that time. But Greg still wasn't sure. The Yankees seemed more than a pitcher away from the World Series. Then he got a call from the Atlanta Braves.

Greg had worked hard to improve his pitching and was rewarded by receiving the 1992 Cy Young Award, which goes to the best pitcher in baseball each season. Here he speaks to reporters with his wife, Kathy.

The Braves had one of the best teams in baseball, having made it to the World Series in both 1991 and 1992, although they were beaten both times. Atlanta already had a trio of young starting pitchers—Tom Glavine, John Smoltz, and Steve Avery. Glavine, in fact, had won the Cy Young Award in 1991, the year before Greg. Team owner Ted Turner felt that the addition of Maddux would keep the Braves in the forefront for years to come. He offered Greg $28 million for five years.

To the surprise of many, Greg took it. He turned down the extra $10 million the Yankees had offered because he liked Atlanta and also liked the fact that he wouldn't be expected to carry the whole team. He would be joining an already successful starting rotation, and would only make it better. "I'm very happy the way things turned out," Greg said. "I'm looking forward to joining a great pitching staff and playing before the fans of Atlanta. I know we all want the same thing—a World Series victory."

When Greg pitched brilliantly in spring training, Manager Bobby Cox tabbed him to be the opening-day starter. Ironically, the Braves would open against the Chicago Cubs at Wrigley Field. Greg would be facing his former teammates.

Not surprisingly, he was booed by the fans who used to cheer him. But he dug in and pitched beautifully. He needed some relief help in the ninth but won the game in a combined shutout. "The booing didn't bother me," Greg said afterward. "I expected that. But it did feel strange pitching against the Cubs in Wrigley after being there all those years. I had knots in my stomach the whole game."

After that, the Braves settled into a season-long rivalry with the San Francisco Giants for first place in the National League Western Division. The Giants led most of the way. Then, with just two days left in the season, the teams

One of Greg's reasons for signing with the Atlanta Braves in 1993 was that he would be joining an elite group of pitchers who had a good chance of leading the team to a World Series victory. From left to right are Tom Glavine, Greg, Pete Smith, John Smoltz, and Steve Avery.

were tied with 102 victories apiece. It was one of the most exciting races in years.

Greg pitched against the Colorado Rockies on the second to last day, holding the hard-hitting team to one run and winning his 20th game of the year. The Giants also won that day, keeping the teams knotted with 103 wins each. "This is what the game is all about," Greg said. "It's exciting. It's also nice to pitch late in the season when every game counts."

On the final day of the season, the Braves won it. Tom Glavine beat the Rockies 5–3, while the Giants were bombed by the Dodgers 12–1. Atlanta would now meet the Philadelphia Phillies, winners of the Eastern Division, in a best-of-seven series with the winner going to the World Series.

The big disappointment came when Atlanta was upset by the Phillies in six games. Greg won the second game for his first play-off win ever. But with his team trailing three games to two, he pitched and lost the sixth game. A line drive that hit him in the leg early might have hampered his pitching, but he made no excuses. "I still think we're the better team," he said. "But [the Phillies] won it and you have to give them credit. Our goal is to win the World Series. This year we didn't get there."

THE BEST THERE IS

After the end of the 1993 season Greg learned he had won the Cy Young Award for a second straight year. Only three pitchers before him—Sandy Koufax, Jim Palmer, and Roger Clemens—had won it two years in a row.

Greg had been proving all along that a pitcher doesn't have to have a blazing fastball to be dominant. In the upcoming two seasons, he would prove it many times over again. In fact, he would put together a pair of seasons that would not only mark him as the best in the game, but as an all-time great as well.

Even before the 1994 season began, Greg had reason to celebrate. In December, his wife gave birth to their first child, Amanda Paige. When spring training began, Greg was in a great frame of mind. He looked forward to another big year and hopefully a trip to the World Series.

There was a big change in the game's structure in 1994. Both leagues had been broken into three divisions—East, Central, and West. There would now be three division winners and a wild-card team (the second-place team with the best record) making the play-offs in each. That would give the sport an extra play-off round and get more teams involved with a chance to go to the World Series. The change in alignment also moved the Braves from the National League West to the National League East.

Greg began pitching brilliantly right from the start. He treated each hitter differently, as if he knew the strengths and weaknesses of all of them. When he wasn't pitching, he wore a pair of round-rimmed glasses that made him look more like an intellectual than an athlete. Early in his career, his nickname had been Mad Dog. Now, his teammates called him The Professor.

By the All-Star break Greg had an incredible 11–2 record and an earned run average that was way under 2.00. He was virtually untouchable. But there was a dark cloud hanging over baseball in 1994. The Players Association and the owners did not have a new labor agreement. The players finally said that if an agreement wasn't reached by August 12, they would go on strike.

That's exactly what happened. On August 12, Greg shut out the Colorado Rockies on three hits for his 16th victory of the year. The next day there was no baseball. Most thought it would be a short strike with an agreement reached quickly. But neither side would compromise and to the surprise of everyone, the remainder of the season was canceled. There would be no World Series for the first time in more than ninety years.

At the time of the strike, Greg had a 16–6 record and a 1.56 earned run average. He led the league in both categories. In 202 innings, he had 156 strikeouts and only 31 walks. He also completed 10 of his 25 starts. Despite the fact that the season had ended early, individual awards were still given out. It came as no surprise when Greg won the Cy Young Award for a record third straight season.

Because the strike of 1994 wasn't settled until the spring of 1995, the new season started in late April and would consist of just 144 games instead of the usual 162. The Braves would run away with the National League East, putting distance between themselves and the other teams right from the start. And once again, Greg Maddux was pitching the kind of baseball rarely seen in the big leagues.

On May 29 he pitched a brilliant one-hitter against the Houston Astros, giving up a home run to Jeff Bagwell and nothing more. He threw only 97 pitches and allowed just four balls to be hit out of the infield. That was becoming the typical Maddux game. He worked fast, walked few, got the job done, and left with another low-scoring win. By the first week in August he had a 12–1 record and a 1.74 earned run average.

He found himself being compared with some of the greatest right-handed pitchers who ever lived. One major sports magazine feature story about him referred to him as, "the best right-handed pitcher born in the past one hundred years."

Greg, indeed, had become a complete student of pitching, a brilliant thinker on the mound who specialized in making good pitches. His fastball moved and darted, and he could throw it anywhere he wanted. Neither his fastball, curve, nor slider were dominant pitches, yet the way he mixed them and controlled them made them extremely hard to hit.

Greg remembered everything. He knew hitters' strengths and weaknesses, and recalled the sequence of pitches he had used against them in the past. As he once said, "In order to be a good pitcher, you've got to think like a hitter. Why do you think I sit beside our hitting coach every game when I'm not pitching?"

Greg looked for every edge, every advantage. Fellow starter Tom Glavine, himself a star, saw Greg as something special. "I think he's got a gift," Glavine said. "He's able to notice things in the course of a game that no one else can— the way a hitter may open up a little, move up in the box an inch, change his stance. I've tried to be aware of that stuff. I really have. But I'm so focused on what *I'm* trying to do. I don't know how he does it."

Through it all, Greg maintained a low profile. He was one of the few sports superstars who didn't have a single major product endorsement. His multimillion dollar contract was more than enough for him. He preferred to keep an aura of mystery about himself as a person. The main reason was his pitching. "A hitter will get, say, six hundred at bats over a year," Greg said. "He may see me only six or seven times out of those six hundred. I'm not going to do anything or say anything that makes him remember me."

In 1995, Greg never looked back. The Braves won their division by a full twenty-one games over the second-place New York Mets, and Greg Maddux had another absolutely brilliant season. He finished the regular season with an incredible 19–2 record and a league-best 1.63 earned run average. In 209.2 innings he had 181 strikeouts and walked only 23 hitters.

With the new play-off setup the Braves first defeated the wild-card Colorado Rockies three games to one, then swept the Cincinnati Reds in four straight to make it to the World Series against the American League Cleveland Indians. Now Greg would have a chance to achieve his longtime dream of helping his team win the World Series.

A CHAMPIONSHIP AND BEYOND

After Greg won the opening game of the 1995 World Series with his masterful two-hitter, the Braves became even bigger favorites to take it all. When Tom Glavine won game two, the Braves were in the driver's seat. Cleveland managed to win the third game before Steve Avery pitched the Braves to a 5–2 triumph in game four. Leading 3–1, the Braves sent Greg back out to the mound to try to wrap up the championship.

Greg didn't pitch quite as well as he had in the first game. The Indians got two runs in the first inning, then two more in the sixth. Greg came out of the game after the seventh, having given up four hits. Cleveland hung on to win 5–4. Tom Glavine was set to pitch in the sixth game, and Greg had some advice for him. "Tommy was wondering if the Indians hitters were adjusting to our off-speed stuff," Greg said. "He began talking about throwing more fastballs than usual. I told him I didn't think the Indians were adjusting. I was just off a little bit, so it wasn't them, it was me. I told him to go out and pitch his game. And whatever he did, don't change."

Glavine took the advice to heart and pitched eight innings, giving up just one hit. Reliever Mark Wohlers pitched the ninth, and a David Justice home run in the sixth was all the scoring. But it was enough. Atlanta won the game 1–0 and the Braves were finally world champs! "This is what I've always worked for,"

Not only can Greg focus on his pitches, he has an amazing ability to remember each batter's strengths and weaknesses and "think like a batter." This ability helped him lead his team past the Colorado Rockies in the first round of the 1995 playoffs. Here, he faces down a Rockies batter.

Greg said. "[Winning the World Series] feels even better than I thought it would. It's the ultimate."

But there was more. After the Series ended, Greg was once again named the Cy Young Award winner in the National League. Incredibly, it was the fourth straight year he had won. He had set a record that should stand for a long time.

At the beginning of the 1996 season, Greg was still just twenty-nine years old. He had never experienced arm trouble and seemed to be getting better and better. But in the 1996 season he wasn't quite as sharp and didn't always get the breaks. He went 15–11 with a 2.72 earned run average. But he still fanned 172 hitters in 245 innings and walked just 28.

With John Smoltz taking up the slack with a 24–8 season, the Braves were again division champs and fought their way back to the World Series. This time they would be facing the team that had wanted Greg in 1993, the New York Yankees. Atlanta was the favorite to repeat, and when they easily won the opening game 12–1 at Yankee Stadium behind John Smoltz, they looked to be on their way.

Greg took the mound in game two, opposed by Yankee veteran Jimmy Key. Key pitched well, but Greg was masterful. When the smoke cleared, the Braves had won 4–0, with Greg giving up just six hits in eight innings. Not surprisingly, he didn't walk a single man. Everyone in New York was impressed.

Greg looks as though he's puzzled at giving up four hits in the third inning of game six of the 1996 World Series. The Yankees seized this opportunity by pulling ahead and winning both the game and the Series.

Yankee manager Joe Torre couldn't say enough about the pitcher who seemed to handcuff his big hitters. "He's the most remarkable pitcher I've seen," Torre said, "in that every time you don't take a swing it's a strike, and every time you do swing, it's a ball. It's like he knows whether the hitter is going to swing."

With the Braves up by two games and heading back to Atlanta, they were expected to win easily. But there was no quit in the Yanks. The Bronx Bombers won games three and four to tie the series. Then, in the pivotal fifth game, Yankee left-hander Andy Pettitte bested John Smoltz in a classic 1–0 pitching duel. Now it was back to New York with the Yankees leading the series 3–2. The home team had not yet won a game.

Greg was on the hill for the Braves. Again, he pitched well . . . except for one inning. In the Yankee third, Paul O'Neill doubled and Joe Girardi tripled, followed by singles from Derek Jeter and Bernie Williams. Just like that, the Yanks had three runs.

It would be enough. Greg went seven and two-thirds innings and gave up nothing else. But the Braves managed just a pair of runs and came up short 3–2. It was the Yankees' turn to be world champs. But a New York sportswriter summed up the almost universal respect for Greg when he began his summation of the final game this way: "Returning home on a wave of emotion after sweeping three games in Atlanta . . . the Yanks went out and beat the best pitcher in the game, Maddux, to sew up their twenty-third World Championship." Even in defeat, Greg was considered the best.

The next generation of Maddux baseball pros? Greg's son Chase pitches to his big sister Amanda Paige, as Dad looks on, before a game with the St. Louis Cardinals in August 1998.

PITCHING FOR PERFECTION

Everyone knew coming into the 1997 season that the Braves had the best team in the National League. Steve Avery had moved on, but lefty Denny Neagle had joined the trio of Maddux, Smoltz, and Glavine to continue to give the team the best starting rotation in the league.

In his personal life, Greg continued to maintain a low profile. In April he and Kathy had their second child, a son they named Chase Alan. In his baseball career, he wanted to keep pitching and winning. When asked if it would be possible to improve on an already outstanding record like his, Greg's answer was a quick yes. "You can be more consistent with your mental approach," he explained, "and the things you do physically on the mound. Instead of making five good pitches an inning, try to make six. You can always do more of what you are doing well."

That's what Greg did in 1997. Once again he was putting together an incredible year. He pitched one of his April victories in one hour and forty-seven minutes, the fastest major-league game in five years. Greg then started the 1997 All-Star Game against Seattle's Randy Johnson, a 6-foot-10-inch (208-centimeter) pitcher known as the "Big Unit" with a blazing fastball and an intimidating presence. But even Johnson acknowledged that Greg was something special. "Even though [Greg and I] are two different extremes, I can still learn a lot from him by how he sets up hitters and his feel for the game," Johnson said. "Without a doubt, Greg is probably the best pitcher to play in the last seven or eight years in the major leagues."

With a 15–3 record by the second week in August, Greg received another reward. This one was in the form of a five-year contract extension worth an amazing $57.5 million. At the time, it made him baseball's highest-paid player.

Greg finished the year with a 19–4 record and a 2.20 earned run average. The Braves won the division again and hoped for a third straight trip to the World Series. They beat Houston in the division series, as Greg threw a seven-hit shut-out. Then, the unthinkable happened. Atlanta was upset by the wild-card Florida Marlins in the National League Championship Series.

Many thought Greg would win a fifth Cy Young Award, but he lost out to Montreal's Pedro Martinez, who had a dominant season. Martinez's record was just 17–8, but his 305 strikeouts and 1.90 earned run average gave him the nod. Greg finished second.

Coming into the 1998 season, the thirty-one-year-old Maddux had a 184–118 record. Many began to feel that he could achieve one of the rarest of baseball milestones—300 career victories. Greg admitted it was possible, but was re-luctant to make any predictions. "Obviously, [300 wins] is a great accomplish-ment because it means you've been good for a long time," Greg said. "Yeah, it's possible, but I would say highly unlikely."

Others didn't feel that way. Former pitcher Rick Sutcliffe pointed to Greg's durability and his pitching motion. "Mechanically, he's as sound as they come," Sutcliffe said. "He's simplified the art of delivering a baseball. He's real delib-erate and fluid, so he puts the least possible stress on his shoulder."

At the end of May, Greg won his seventh game of the year, going eight and one-third innings in a 2–0 win over Montreal. Pitching in relief for the

Expos was his brother, Mike. Greg got to hit against him for just the seventh time in his career and grounded to the shortstop. "That was fun," Greg said afterward. "I would rather have gotten one hit against him than two hits against the other guy."

Mike had not found nearly the same success Greg had. He was a pitcher of average ability, able to start or relieve, and he had changed teams many times just to stay in the big leagues. But the brothers remained close and, when possible, competitive.

After Greg's first 25 starts of the season he had run his record to 15–5 with a 1.53 ERA. He seemed on course for an unprecedented fifth Cy Young Award. As usual, the Braves were once again leading their division. Then, for one of the first times in his career, Greg lost a bit of his magic. Though the team coasted home with another division title, Greg limped home by going 3–4 in his final starts.

"I didn't locate [my pitches] as well as I would have liked [late in the season]," Greg said before the playoffs began. "But I'm pleased with how I've thrown lately, so it doesn't matter. What matters is how I pitch the next game."

Although his name may not be instantly recognizable to millions and he is not the flashiest pitcher in baseball, Greg Maddux is well respected by the baseball world, including fellow pitchers, and is considered to be one of the best of all time. He is pictured here with teammate Chipper Jones.

As usual, Greg didn't dwell on the past, even the immediate past. He managed to finish the 1998 season with an 18–9 mark and a 2.22 earned run average, almost the identical ERA as his 19–4 season the year before. He struck out more than 200 hitters (204) for the first time in his career, had 5 shutouts (a career best), and 9 complete games. And his 16th victory of the season was also the 200th of his career. It was still a super year, although teammate Tom Glavine would win the Cy Young, his second.

The Braves, however, suffered a disappointment in the play-offs. They beat the Cubs in the division series, but lost to the San Diego Padres in the championship series. Once again, they failed to make it to the World Series. As great as Greg and the Braves had been for so many years, they had won the World Series just once.

The 1999 Braves were again favored to win the National League East and continued to be looked upon as one of the elite teams in all of baseball. The club, however, lost power-hitting first baseman Andres Galarraga (44 homers and 121 RBIs in 1998) for the season with a cancerous growth in his back. He hoped to return for the 2000 season. Part of the slack was taken up by hard-hitting outfielder Brian Jordan, who signed as a free agent, and with the big three still on the mound—Tom Glavine, John Smoltz, and Greg Maddux—the Braves continued to be a threat to win it all. Greg started the season where he left off, pitching extremely well and winning his first two games.

There are still goals to reach for this intelligent, laid-back pitcher. Off the field, Greg and his wife, Kathy, head up the Maddux Foundation, which is connected to a number of charitable activities. Among other things, they donate Braves tickets to nonprofit organizations.

Greg Maddux doesn't throw as hard as some pitchers. He doesn't have a physically intimidating presence on the mound. He doesn't strike out three hundred batters a year. But he wins games—and he does it with a kind of flair all his own, making even the best hitters look like beginners. When Greg Maddux is on his game and putting his pitches where he wants them, he's virtually untouchable—a master on the mound and one of the best of all time.

GREG MADDUX: HIGHLIGHTS

1966   Born on April 14 in San Angelo, Texas.

1976   Family moves to Las Vegas, Nevada. Along with older brother, Mike, develops baseball skills under the guidance of Rusty Medar.

1983   Pitching and playing center field for Valley High School, named to All-State team.

1984   Selected in second round of the draft by the Chicago Cubs.
Joins single-A team at Pikeville, North Carolina.

1986   Moves up to double-A team at Pittsfield, Massachusetts.
Promoted to triple-A level at Iowa.
Joins the Chicago Cubs roster in the major leagues.

1990   Wins first Gold Glove Award.

1992   Wins first Cy Young Award.
Pitches in first All-Star Game.
Becomes a free agent at the end of the season and signs with the Atlanta Braves.

1993   Wins Cy Young Award for the second straight year.
Takes fourth straight Gold Glove Award.

1994   Is starting pitcher in the All-Star Game.
Becomes the first pitcher ever to win three consecutive Cy Young Awards.

1995   Captures fourth straight Cy Young Award.
Braves defeat the Cleveland Indians in the World Series.

1996   Wins seventh straight Gold Glove Award.

1998   Strikes out 204 batters and finishes with an 18–9 record and a 2.22 ERA.
Pitches two hundred or more innings for the eleventh straight year.

FIND OUT MORE

Christopher, Matt. *On the Mound With Greg Maddux*. Boston: Little, Brown, 1997.

Gay, Douglas, and Kathlyn Gay. *The Not-So-Minor Leagues*. Brookfield, CT: Millbrook, 1996.

Macht, Norman L. *Cy Young*. Broomall, PA: Chelsea House, 1992.

Sehnert, Chris W. *Top 10 Pitchers*. Minneapolis: ABDO, 1997.

Thornley, Stew. *Sports Great Greg Maddux*. Springfield, NJ: Enslow, 1997.

How to write to Greg Maddux:

Greg Maddux

c/o Atlanta Braves

P.O. Box 4064

Atlanta, GA 30302

Braves Website:

www.atlantabraves.com

INDEX